CONTENTS

Serving as a Greeter or Usher 1

Greeters 13

Ushers 19

Creating, Leading, and Sustaining a Ministry of Welcome 29

Appendix 38

SERVING AS A GREETER OR USHER

Introduction

One summer, I took a misstep on a flight of stairs on the last night of vacation and broke my foot. I spent eight weeks in a boot and had to use a knee scooter to get around. About two weeks into this experience, my husband and I were debating whether we could still attend a concert we'd been looking forward to for months. It was being held at a large arena in downtown Kansas City, and I was nervous about navigating the city and the crowds at the arena with my scooter.

I decided to call the Guest Services department at the arena and ask if they thought I would have difficulty. The representative I spoke to (yes, a real person, not a recording) assured me, "We are well-prepared to meet your needs. Please have no worries about it whatsoever. When you arrive, a Guest Services greeter will meet you at the entrance, and our team will escort you all the way to your seat. We'll take great care of you." We decided to attend the concert, but I'll admit to being just a little skeptical about receiving a personal escort in a giant arena.

On the evening of the concert, as my husband and I approached the arena entrance, a young man waved us over to his door. He told us he had noticed my scooter and would assist us through the required metal detectors and ensure our experience was comfortable. Once through that process, he directed us to a person wearing a Guest Services shirt standing about twenty feet away, who was smiling and waving to us. She welcomed us and walked with us to an elevator that would take us to the floor level of the arena, where our seats were located. She introduced us to the elevator operator, who explained that someone would meet us at the elevator doors to escort us directly to our seats.

We were already blown away by the excellent service we'd received. When the elevator arrived on our floor, the woman who met us there (Sandy) explained that she would take us to our seats and then take the scooter to a little "garage" so it wouldn't be an impediment to other foot traffic in the arena. She showed us where that was and told us we could retrieve it at any time, and then she identified for us the closest restrooms. She explained that ushers would be walking up and down the aisles during the entire concert, and that if I needed to use the restroom or go to the concession stand, I should simply ask one of them and they'd bring my scooter to me. I noticed other ushers providing the same service to a man on crutches seated in the row behind us and a woman in a wheelchair seated one section over. About five minutes before the break between bands, I asked an usher to bring me the scooter, and he pointed me toward a restroom that would have a shorter line. Toward the end of the concert, Sandy tapped me on the shoulder, showed us that she'd brought the scooter to the end of our aisle, and informed us that there were four songs left in the concert. If we wanted to make our way to the vestibule where we entered, we could watch the end of the concert from there and then be escorted all the way out instead of fighting the crowd to exit.

I lead the ministries of hospitality and connection at my local church in Leawood, Kansas, Resurrection: A United Methodist Church. We constantly strive for great hospitality, and still I was amazed by the level of welcome and service that I received at that concert. The greeters and ushers at this arena made us feel welcome and comfortable, and they anticipated and met every need we had. I couldn't wait to share the story of this experience with my team, because it illustrated to me the kind of welcome we work so hard to provide to guests through our ushers and greeters at church. I have talked to my friends, coworkers, and volunteers more about the excellence of the greeters and ushers at this arena than I have the actual concert we attended.

We use the term *guests* to refer to every person who walks in our doors. Some of those are first-time guests, some are members who worship regularly, and some are folks who attend on occasion—but we want them all to feel like we've been preparing for and anticipating their arrival with much excitement. We all come to church with hopes and needs, joys and worries. Being welcomed warmly and made to feel safe and comfortable enables our guests to transition smoothly from the stress and strains of daily life to an environment and mindset in which they can encounter God in a meaningful way.

Ushers and greeters are a critical part of the worship experience. In most cases, the first (and sometimes only) personal interaction a guest has during their first visit at a new church is with an usher or a greeter, and they can make or break a guest's experience. It takes guests about thirty seconds to form a first impression of your church, and they'll decide within seven to ten minutes whether or not they want to return.[1] That's long before the first worship song is sung, a word of prayer has been spoken, or the pastor has had a chance to deliver his or her sermon. It means, in effect, that the welcome guests receive from the greeters and ushers will likely have a greater impact on their decision to return than the pastor's message does. Excellent greeters and ushers make a difference!

In this handbook, I'll share guidelines for serving with excellence as an usher or greeter and share some tips and resources for leading effective usher and greeter teams. In some churches, ushers and greeters are the same position, but in many these are different roles, and for that reason I'll discuss these roles separately. An Appendix includes Usher and Greeter position descriptions, Head Usher and Greeter position descriptions, and the Volunteer Covenant that we use at Resurrection.

Defining Ushers Versus Greeters

In many smaller churches, everyone involved wears multiple hats, including the people who serve as ushers and greeters. This is not usually a challenge if your space is smaller and has one or two points of entry. For churches that meet in larger spaces, whether that's a school gym, a movie theater, or a large auditorium, it's more common for volunteers to specialize in specific roles while they're serving. For the purpose of this handbook, I'm going to describe these functions separately to provide clarity, but we'll spend a little time below talking about the things they have in common.

In most churches where these roles are distinct, the term *Greeters* is used to describe those volunteers who serve as the first impression for the church. Typically, they serve outside the worship or event space: in the parking lot, at the entry doors to the building, and in the lobby area. Theirs are the first faces guests see, and their smiles are the first smiles a guest receives. Their role sets the stage for the guest's entire experience, and their primary ministry is one of welcome.

Ushers usually serve inside the event or worship space, starting at the entrance doors to that space. Their ministry is one of welcome, too, but they also have responsibility for implementing worship elements such as attendance (if your church takes attendance), offering, Communion, and providing a safe and secure worship or event experience.

What Do Great Ushers and Greeters Have in Common?

The best ushers and greeters make it their mission to make others feel welcome. They go out of their way to make guests comfortable. They are friendly, attentive, and prepared to serve. They practice the three Principles of Excellent Hospitality: **Notice**, **Offer Personal Attention**, and **Provide Excellent Follow-Through**.

The principle of **Notice** involves both social and situational awareness. Who is around you? What are they doing? Do they look lost or in need of assistance? What is happening around you? Is there a spill that needs to be cleaned up? Maybe a messy stack of bulletins that needs to be tidied? Is the trash can overflowing and in need of being emptied?

In order to notice, you can't be rushing. When we're rushing, we are so focused on what we need to do next that we aren't aware of who or what is around us. Excellent ushers and greeters arrive early to serve so they can be ready to notice.

Noticing means offering a warm greeting to the people you encounter. This can be a smile, a simple "Good Morning!" or "Good to see you today!" Being on the lookout for issues in the environment or facilities is also an important part of noticing. This helps us maintain a clean and well-maintained space, which makes for a better guest experience.

One weekend when I was leading our usher team during Saturday night worship, the service had ended and we were busily tidying our space for the next service. Eileen, one of our ushers, came to me and said she'd noticed three people, an elderly woman and a couple, who had remained in the sanctuary after everyone else had exited. This isn't unusual, and she said no one seemed to be crying or visibly upset, but she said something about the way they were sitting and interacting made her think they might need to talk to a pastor. I called Pastor Joshua, and he approached the group.

Pastor Joshua came to find me after he spoke with the family, a mother and her son and daughter-in-law. They had just received news the day before that the mother's cancer was terminal, she hadn't responded to any of the treatments, and they were out of options. They had never been to our church before, and didn't attend church anywhere, but came seeking hope in the midst of their despair. He prayed with them, offered them some resources that we had available, and set up an appointment to follow up with them. Think about the impact of that. This family, first-time guests, received loving care that they desperately needed simply because one of our ushers had not been rushing, but had noticed them and acted on her observations.

The second principle of Excellent Hospitality is **Offer Personal Attention**, and it starts with the person right in front of you. To do this well, we have to avoid getting caught up in conversations with our friends or fellow volunteers, so we're available to interact directly with people as they enter. Introduce yourself if it's appropriate and learn the other person's name. Then introduce them to others so they build connections that create a sense of community.

One great way to offer personal attention is to practice two rules:

- **The 10-foot rule**: Take responsibility for welcoming those within 10 feet of you anytime you're at church, especially those who are alone.
- **The 3-minute rule**: Spend at least 3 minutes before and after any worship service or church event talking to someone you don't know very well.

One Sunday morning I decided to worship at our Blue Springs location for the first time. I was feeling a little self-conscious as I walked in, so I went to the coffee station to grab a cup of coffee. Much to my surprise, the gentleman in front of me turned around and offered me the cup he had just poured, and then he poured another for himself. I thanked him, we introduced ourselves, and then we parted company. As I sat down in worship, I noticed that the man who'd given me the coffee was right in front of me. We struck up a conversation and learned that we had children the same age who just happened to live within five miles of each other in different states. My son and his daughter both lived in Seattle, and my daughter and his son both lived in Missouri. His wife was serving in our children's ministry while he was in worship. That old saying, "it's a small world," is true. Every time I go to that location, Grant and I exchange a warm hello and spend a minute chatting. I'm grateful that he was willing to spend a few minutes before church initiating conversation with someone he didn't know, because his willingness to do so made me more comfortable in what was a new worship environment for me.

Offering personal attention also means anticipating and fulfilling each guest's needs. For greeters, that may mean assisting a person with limited mobility into the building or covering someone with an umbrella when they're dropped off at the door in the rain. For ushers, it could be providing coloring sheets and crayons to families with small children or making sure there are tissues available during cold and flu season.

The final principle of Excellent Hospitality is **Provide Excellent Follow-Through**. A big part of this principle (for both ushers and greeters) is taking ownership of any issues you notice with guests or the facility and making sure the problem is resolved.

As our 11 a.m. worship service began one Sunday morning, I noticed Kathy, one of our ushers, running up the stairs to the balcony with a roll of paper towels in her hands. Apparently, someone had spilled a cup of coffee and the fluid was dripping down on the people seated below. Kathy didn't wait for anyone else to take care of it; she just grabbed the paper towels herself and ran to clean up the spill (and stop the dripping on the poor souls below). Then she went to the people who had been on the receiving end of the spill and apologized to them. They were kind, laughing it off and thanking her for making it stop.

Excellent follow-through involves finding answers to questions that guests ask and you can't answer in the moment, and then making sure the guests get the answer. Rather than saying, "I don't know," say "I'll find out." It also means offering a warm and sincere goodbye as people depart at the end of a service or an event.

Our ushers stand near the exits as people make their way out of the worship space after the service, telling people goodbye, wishing them a great week, and thanking them for coming. Most people look up, smile, and return the greeting. If we can bring a smile to people's faces when they arrive and when they leave, that's a win.

Who Can Serve as an Usher or a Greeter?

The answer to this question will depend a lot on your church's traditions and norms. In some faith traditions there are rather stringent requirements for who can serve as an usher. For these churches, the role of usher has specific prerequisites and is seen as a solemn responsibility for those who are deeply involved in church leadership.

In others, the threshold for service is more relaxed. At my local church, we invite anyone who has the gift, time, and willingness to serve, as long as they agree to support our church's vision and purpose and fulfill our expectations for serving in these roles.

And yes, this means we invite families with young children to serve together, as well as high schoolers and adults. It may not work everywhere, but we find that it works for us. One doesn't need to be a member of our church in order to serve as a greeter or usher. We are very intentional about this. We believe it's possible for someone to come to church every weekend and still somehow stall out in their faith journey. When people get involved in studying the Bible with others in a small group or serving with others on a volunteer team, their faith comes alive, so we want everyone to get involved in serving. Because young families have a thousand opportunities to do things together on the weekend, from soccer to dance to just staying home, we are purposeful in inviting young people and young families to serve. We are hoping to reverse a trend many churches are seeing today—increasingly, students who disengage from church after high school never come back.

We want high school students to feel comfortable and engaged in worship, to know they are contributing to something bigger than themselves. We believe this will encourage them to stay connected to church into adulthood. For families with young children, allowing them to serve with their kids serves two purposes: it lets them be involved while still being in church with their kiddos, and it models for their children a life of service in the church. When visiting families see other families serving in church, it sends a clear message that your church is family-friendly, which will help them feel more comfortable. One of our most committed families began ushering together about six years ago, when their identical triplet boys were six years old and their daughter was three. At that time the boys ushered with a parent, and their daughter often went to the nursery. Now the boys are almost teenagers and are assigned their own sections to cover, while their sister serves with one of her parents. Wouldn't you love to have a family of six usher together? Sometimes they're half our usher team at their particular service!

Our church has a large ministry for children and adults with special needs, and many of them are able to serve well with their families. We have volunteers with varying levels of physical abilities, and we accommodate them as much as we can. Some can't handle stairs; others need their partner to carry the attendance notebooks, as they can't carry heavy weights. None of these different abilities impact their ability to offer excellent hospitality.

Is There a Dress Code?

Again, this will depend greatly on your local church's preferences and requirements. When I was growing up, everyone dressed up in their "Sunday best" for church. The men wore suits and the women wore dresses. In most churches today the expectations for attire have relaxed significantly, but even in churches where casual dress is common, many people still prefer to dress up for church. In my congregation, we have both contemporary and traditional services. Our contemporary services usually see people dressed very casually, and in our traditional services—even our most traditional service—you're likely to see some people dressed up nicely and others in jeans or casual slacks.

If you're serving as an usher or greeter, your attire should be in alignment with the norms of your church and specific service, with a few caveats. Always arrive clean and neat. Dress respectfully—no revealing or too-tight clothes. This doesn't apply only to women. I know a number of men who are quite proud of their physique and wear clothes designed to emphasize their muscularity. Remember, your goal is to make others comfortable, not to draw attention to yourself. Talk to your team leader to get specific guidelines for attire when serving.

Some churches, ours included, ask volunteers to wear a name tag, T-shirt, or lanyard that makes it easier for guests to identify who they can go to if they need assistance. This is really critical. If an emergency happens, they know they just need to grab the nearest person with a blue T-shirt or lanyard in our church, and they anticipate those people can answer their question and know what to do in an emergency. If your team leader asks you to wear special attire, a lanyard, or a name tag, please do so. Those things also signal to guests that you are prepared for and anticipating their arrival.

I've noticed that when I'm serving and wearing my hospitality team T-shirt, guests are not only more likely to stop me to ask a question but also more likely to accept my offer of assistance when I approach them. The official team attire, whether it's a T-shirt, a name tag, or a lanyard, adds a measure of credibility and authority.

Be careful about wearing too much cologne or perfume when you're serving, as many people are sensitive to or even allergic to certain fragrances. One way to make sure your cologne isn't too strong is to just avoid wearing it when you're serving.

As you interact with guests, fresh breath is important too. We keep a supply of mints on hand for our ushers and greeters for this reason.

Safety and Security

Ushers and greeters play a critical role in maintaining safety and security. These volunteers are the first to welcome guests and create a positive first impression, which means they are in a prime position to notice things that might put people's safety at risk. This can be as simple as papers that have fallen on the floor or a loose piece of carpet, both of which create a slipping or falling hazard. Those are easy to address. Other issues may require expert assistance. This is one of the primary reasons we ask our ushers to wear two-way radios. They can make a call on that radio to the Head Usher, our facilities team, our security team, or our medical team much faster than they can pull out a phone and dial.

Talk through emergency situation plans with your staff liaison or team leader, and make sure every usher knows what to do in case of an emergency, whether that's medical, severe weather, fire, or something more serious. Ninety-nine percent of the safety issues you deal with as an usher or greeter are going to be things you can easily address or find someone else to address without even disrupting service, but always be alert and prepared for anything.

Greeters are often the first to notice when someone or something "just doesn't look right." Always be aware of your surroundings and observant of the people around you. If you have any concern or are simply uncomfortable with something you see, don't try to address it yourself, but instead make the person in charge aware of the situation. We want all volunteers to feel empowered to "see something, say something," so that trained staff or lead volunteers can then "do something." The Cybersecurity and Infrastructure Security Agency produces a great downloadable resource called "The Power of Hello." "The Power of Hello - Houses of Worship Guide" states:

> Simply saying "Hello" can prompt a casual conversation with a new person, providing an opportunity to observe and establish a connection. The OHNO approach–Observe, Initiate a Hello, Navigate the Risk, and Obtain Help–enables staff [and volunteers] to observe and evaluate suspicious behaviors, empowering them to lower risk and obtain help when necessary.[2]

"The Power of Hello" empowers us to lead with hospitality while also ensuring the safety of our congregation.

Ushers are often the first to notice when a worshipper is ill and needs emergency assistance. We've seen this many times—everything from someone scratching themselves on a sharp edge and bleeding to fainting, low blood sugar reactions, and heart attacks. If your church has a medical response team or a security team, call them first so they can assess and stabilize the person. Then, if necessary, call 911. At our largest location, we have a team of doctors and nurses who volunteer their time to be "on call" for these kinds of emergencies during worship. At our other locations, we have only a first aid kit. That means the ushers, along with the staff team, have to assess and make the 911 call. Keep the area around the person clear so that he or she has room to breathe and the medical personnel have space to work. Usually, these incidents aren't life-threatening. However, they can be, so ushers need to be prepared.

Many times, emergencies are not related to one person's health, but to severe weather or fire. In Kansas, where I live, we expect and prepare for tornado season. Every year our security team does a brief reminder training for our ushers, practicing where to lead people in case of severe weather and how to evacuate people out of the building most efficiently in case of a fire or bomb threat. Be aware that as an usher, the congregation sees you as an authority, and they will go where you lead them. Do drills and practice sessions so you feel prepared and can remain calm.

The worst-case scenario for any church is an active shooter. Many churches now have security teams, sometimes off-duty police officers in uniform, to act as a deterrent. I'm not a security expert, but I will share with you what we share with our ushers and greeters. When you arrive to serve and get your assignment, locate the closest exit so you don't have to search for it in a time of crisis. If there is an active shooter situation, call 911, your security team if you have one, and get down. If you're not in the shooter's line of sight and can get people (and yourself) out of the building, do that, but don't endanger more lives by making yourself and others a target. If you can't get out safely, get down and stay down so the police can respond without distraction when they arrive.

NOTES

1. Tyler Schmall, "This Is Exactly How Long You Have to Make a Good First Impression," *New York Post*, December 14, 2018, https://nypost.com/2018/12/14/this-is-exactly-how-long-you-have-to-make-a-good-first-impression/; Jill Bremer, "Seven Minutes and Counting," in *Fusion: Turning First-Time Guests into Fully-Engaged Members of Your Church*, eds. Nelson Searcy and Jennifer Dykes Henson (Grand Rapids: Baker, 2007), 49.
2. Cybersecurity and Infrastructure Security Agency, *The Power of Hello Guide for Houses of Worship* (Capital Heights, MD: CISA, 2022), https://www.cisa.gov/sites/default/files/2022-11/The%20Power%20of%20Hello%20Guide%20for%20Houses%20of%20Worship_508.pdf.

GREETERS

Preparing to Serve

Mark your calendar for the weeks and services at which you're scheduled to serve. Make sure you allow plenty of time to leave home so you can arrive well before your time to serve. We ask our greeters to arrive forty minutes before their worship service starts. This allows them a few minutes to put away their coats, umbrellas, or handbags and to be ready to meet with their Head Greeter for their huddle.

The Huddle is a five- to ten-minute stand-up gathering with their Head Greeter and other greeters on their team where they can hear any important updates for the weekend, get their door assignments, share their joys and concerns with one another, and pray specifically that they will represent the love of Jesus exceptionally well to every person they encounter. This quick check-in settles greeters' hearts and prepares them to be a welcoming presence to our guests.

Then they're ready to grab a greeter badge and any tools they need (gloves if it's cold, sunglasses if it's hot and sunny, umbrellas if it's raining) and get into their positions before guests begin to arrive. Our goal is for greeters to be in position twenty-five to thirty minutes before the service starts, so they're able to greet the first arrivals. Talk to your team leader about his or her expectations for when you should be in position and ready to serve. Every church context is a little different.

We assign our greeters to serve in pairs at our higher-traffic doors, so if one needs to leave to escort a new person somewhere, the door isn't left without a greeter. In addition to our exterior doors, we're also trying to position greeters indoors at any decision point, where a guest needs to decide whether to go one way or another, so our greeters can help them find their desired location. For instance, our children's space is on the opposite side of the building from our busiest entrance. Having a greeter stationed just inside that space allows them to notice and be available when guests look like they need assistance navigating to the children's area. We also have simultaneous services at 11 a.m. on Sundays in separate buildings, and we try to position a greeter at either end of the hallway that connects those two buildings so they can help guests find their way to the service they want to attend.

Guest Arrival

As guests begin to pull into the parking lot, our greeters stand outside the outer doors to be ready to welcome those arriving. Think about how you would greet a guest at home. You wouldn't expect them to open the door for themselves; you'd greet them at the door, welcoming them personally. We need to provide that personal welcome at church too. Greeters should smile, offer a warm greeting, and open the doors for guests as they approach. Please don't underestimate the power of your smile to transform someone's mood.

I was greeting at our west doors one brutally hot Saturday afternoon, with my sunglasses on, sweat soaking through my T-shirt that said, "We're Glad You're Here!" I smiled and opened the door for a guest who was walking up with a miserable expression on her face (it was VERY hot!), and I said to her, "It's so good to see you! There's plenty of A/C waiting for you inside." She laughed and replied, "Thank you for being out here to welcome me. I'm glad to be here!" A very simple interaction, but she walked in with a smile on her face, where before there hadn't been one.

If you know someone's name, use it. Dale Carnegie said, "Remember that a person's name is to that person the sweetest and most important sound in any language."[1] It's true. We all want to feel seen and known. When I walk into my local grocery store, I always go to the same cashier if I can—Don—because he greets me by name, and it makes me feel good!

Remember not to get caught up in conversations with your friends or fellow greeters. You want to be able to focus all your attention on the people coming in. Pay attention to guests' body language as they arrive. Some will be looking at their phone or otherwise intentionally avoiding eye contact. This means they don't want to engage, and we need to respect that. Still, smile warmly and offer a brief welcome before moving your attention to the next person. Others will smile broadly and approach with their hand out for a handshake or arms out for a hug. Shake hands gently if they initiate the handshake, but don't expect every person to shake hands. Remember that some guests may have arthritis or may just not like a firm grip, while others might have their own reasons for not wanting to shake hands at all. Hopefully if someone reaches out for a hug, it's a person you know well. If not, turn and offer a brief "side hug" if you're comfortable doing so, or turn and use both hands to hold the door open while smiling. You shouldn't initiate hugs, and you shouldn't feel required to accept anyone else's hug, either.

It's important to offer special assistance to those in a wheelchair or on crutches, if needed, along with anyone else who might have special needs. Make sure you acknowledge children as they arrive, offering a smile and a wave or a high-five. Bend down to look them in the eye if you're comfortable doing so. Guests notice when we notice their loved ones.

If you notice a person or family stop and look around when they get inside, you might simply ask, "Can I help you find something?" Don't assume they're new, but they may need directions. If they need help finding a specific location, and you're working with a partner, escort the guest to their location while your partner stays in position. Once you've shown the guest to their location, return to your greeter position. If you don't have a partner, direct them to another volunteer or staff person, or even another guest you know.

Ann and Don are members of my church who shared with us the story of their first visit. As they arrived, the greeter, Bill, opened the door and welcomed them. They asked him for directions to the sanctuary. This told Bill that they were new guests. Bill was serving alone at his door, so he asked them if they would wait for just a moment because he recognized another couple approaching the door and knew they were regulars. He introduced the members to the new couple and asked the regulars if they would escort the guests to the sanctuary. They did, but first they gave Ann and Don a little tour, got them a cup of coffee, and invited them to sit with them. Ann told us that she and Don decided that day that they wanted to be part of our church.

During Worship

We ask our greeters to stay at their doors to welcome guests through the first fifteen minutes of the service. What that means is once a month, when our greeters serve, they miss much of the worship music and walk in midway through the worship service. The same is true for greeters who serve during our weekly programming. We ask them to stay in position until fifteen minutes after the program starts. Why do we do that? Because the people arriving late are frequently first-time guests, who either got the start time of the event wrong or had trouble finding the location or parking. They're arriving already stressed out because they're late. We want them to know that we are (still) ready and waiting for them and that they are welcome whatever time they arrive. A kind word of encouragement and welcome can transform their tension about being late into anticipation for the upcoming experience.

Fifteen minutes into the worship service or program, our greeters return their greeter badges and any supplies they used, then join the service or event as participants.

Post-Service

It's a nice touch for greeters to head back to their positions during the benediction in worship or the closing comments in a ministry program, to be ready to offer a warm and sincere goodbye to guests. Once guests have exited, gather with your team for a quick debrief of any situations that arose that others should be aware of and to share stories of ministry impact.

Special Services

Greeters are frequently asked to serve at special events or services. This may be a special worship service, such as Ash Wednesday, or an event with a guest speaker that's open to the community. Keep in mind that guests' first encounter with your church can be a special event, a serving opportunity, or regular programming as well as weekend worship. It's tremendously helpful to have greeters at every event, not only to provide that warm welcome, but also practically, to be able to guide people who might not be familiar with your church to their desired location.

Dress appropriately and align the tone of your greeting for these special occasions. For instance, at our Good Friday prayer vigil and our Ash Wednesday service, we ask our greeters to be warm and friendly but to keep in mind that these are more somber events and to keep their voices low and dress accordingly.

Tips for Greeting with Excellence

- Arrive on time; your leader is counting on you.
- Dress appropriately for the weather and stand outside to welcome guests.
- Smile—you are the first person a guest will encounter at your church.
- Open doors for guests.
- Greet everyone warmly.
- Offer a hand to those people needing extra assistance getting inside.
- If you are greeting with a partner, escort guests who ask for directions to their location, and then return to your door.
- Remain at your door until fifteen minutes after the service begins.

- Return to your door to offer a warm and sincere goodbye as guests leave.

Greeters are the face of the church for those who come. An authentic welcome and a warm smile can transform someone's day. People come to church with all sorts of needs, expectations, and occasionally something weighing heavily on their hearts. They may be coming back to church after a long absence. Your role as a greeter is vital to making people feel accepted and welcomed, to feel like they could belong. And that's the first step in faith, because before anyone decides to get connected into a church or grow in their faith, they first have to feel like they could belong.

NOTE

1. Dale Carnegie, *How to Win Friends and Influence People* (New York: Simon & Schuster, 1981), 105.

USHERS

Preparing to Serve

As mentioned for Greeters, mark your calendar for the weeks and services at which you're scheduled to serve. Your Head Usher or staff leader is counting on you, and honoring your commitment to serve as scheduled will be greatly appreciated.

Make sure you allow plenty of time to leave home so you can arrive well before your time to serve. We ask our ushers to arrive thirty minutes before their worship service starts. This allows them time to put away their things, make sure the supplies they need are in place in their assigned sections, and be ready to meet with their Head Usher for their huddle.

The Huddle is a five- to ten-minute stand-up gathering with their Head Usher and other ushers on their team where they can hear the order of service and any important updates for the weekend, get their door assignments (if applicable), share their joys and concerns with one another, and pray specifically that they will reflect Christ's love to each person they encounter. Like our greeter huddle, this is a great tool for putting persons in the right frame of mind and preparing them to be a welcoming presence to our guests.

After the huddle, they grab an usher badge, a radio, and any supplies they need; do a quick check to make sure their section is tidy; and get into their position before guests begin to arrive.

Before guests begin to arrive, find a seat for yourself near your section. We ask our members to pick seats in the middle of the row and leave the seats on the end for guests or others arriving later, but serving as an usher is an exception. You want to find a seat from which you can easily get in and out to complete your duties, so select a seat on the end toward the back of your section. Our goal is for ushers to be in position twenty minutes before the service starts, because this is when we open our sanctuary doors.

It is with intention that we keep the doors of the worship spaces closed while our worship leaders rehearse, the pastors do microphone checks, and our acolytes practice. We want the space to feel sacred and distraction-free when guests enter. Your church may or may not do this. One thing to keep in mind if your church doesn't have a specific time to open the doors—you'll need to be in your position sooner. Ask your team leader what time you should plan to arrive to serve.

Guest Arrival

Some ushers are assigned to hand out bulletins at doors, while others are assigned to greet guests inside the worship space. At Resurrection, my home church, we no longer print bulletins, but we did before COVID-19. We assigned our ushers to serve in pairs or teams to pass out bulletins, so if one needed to leave to escort a guest somewhere, the door wasn't left without an usher. Most frequently our guests are looking for the children's ministry space or the restrooms. Like with our greeters, if our ushers can escort rather than point to a location, it provides a higher standard of service.

When you're handing out bulletins at the doors, don't get caught up in conversation with your friends or fellow ushers, but rather actively engage in welcoming guests who are entering. If a guest needs additional assistance getting to a seat or finding a spot to accommodate a wheelchair, introduce them to an usher inside the space, who can then escort them to a seat.

One important note: as people are entering or you're greeting people near your section, avoid touching anyone. Don't put your hand on their shoulder, elbow, or back. If a guest extends their hand, naturally you can shake their hand, but be aware that some people are very uncomfortable being touched. Be mindful of others' personal space. In the United States, most people feel that anyone standing closer than arm's length away is invading their space. In other cultures, the personal space norm is smaller or larger. Notice people's body language. If they step back or lean their neck back when you're talking to them, you are invading their space.

In some churches, ushers are asked to actively seat people as they enter. Typically, in a church with this expectation, ushers will try to seat people near the front of the space first and fill in toward the back. At Resurrection, we ask our ushers to stand facing the doors near their sections, smile and welcome people as they arrive, and ask if they need help finding a seat. Most of the time our guests will respond that they don't need (or want) assistance, but occasionally they take us up on the offer. At that point we ask if they have a preferred area to sit in and if they do, we work hard to get them as close to that section as possible. If your church provides coloring sheets or other toys for children, offer those to families as they enter.

At both Christmas and Easter, we do actively seat people. On those two holidays, most of our services are at capacity, so we encourage our ushers to work together to help people find seats. The ushers near the entrances will tell guests entering where the most available seats are located. If a guest tells them they have four people in their party, we ask our ushers to make eye contact with their fellow ushers while holding up four fingers, and look for a teammate who will respond by indicating that they have four seats together in their section by holding up four fingers in response. When that happens, the first usher directs the party to the usher with the seats, who then escorts the group to their seats.

During Worship

Ushers are not only on the front line of hospitality; they also play a critical role in making sure the worship service runs smoothly. Ushers in most churches are tasked with collecting the offering and doing a head count in their sections. In my church, ushers also assist with the flow of Communion.

Some guests will arrive late, after worship has started. Most of the time they had every intention to arrive on time but still find themselves walking into worship five or ten minutes into the service. Often these are guests who didn't accurately estimate the travel time to your location or from the parking lot or how long it would take to check their children into your children's programming. Don't make them feel guilty for arriving late; they are already stressed about it. Make sure they feel welcome. If they arrive during prayer, if you have your head bowed and eyes closed, most will take their cue from you and wait until the prayer ends before finding a seat. If they don't, let them go. If they do wait, once the prayer ends, turn and welcome them with a smile and a quiet greeting and ask if they need help finding a seat or show them where they can easily find one.

Attendance

Your church may or may not track attendance in worship. Some churches have pew pads that are meant to be passed down the row at some point. Other churches track attendance using connect cards that are placed in seatbacks or passed in baskets. Many churches only ask guests to complete a connect card, while others ask everyone in worship to complete one. I've seen three different means of collecting these: they are placed in the offering plates or baskets as they're passed, guests are instructed to take them to a specific location after the service (and often incentivized to do so with the offer of a free gift), or they are asked to hand them to an usher after the service.

Pre-COVID-19, we passed attendance notebooks as a separate element in each of our worship services. Typically, this element came about fifteen or twenty minutes into the service so we could include those who arrived late. The pastor would say something like this from the chancel:

> I'm going to invite our ushers forward, and they'll be handing you our attendance notebooks. Your presence today is very important to us. Please sign in and let us know you were here. Once you've signed in, pass it down the row. When it reaches the end of the row, pass it back. As it comes to you a second time, open it up and look for the names of the persons seated

on your right and left, so you can greet them by name after the service. If you're a guest with us, welcome. We are so glad you're here. There is a welcome brochure on the left-hand side for you to take with you that will give you more information about our church.

Then our ushers would bring the attendance notebooks forward. We asked them to turn the notebooks, so they are facing the guest and ready to be opened when they hand them to the first person on each row. When the pandemic hit and worship was all online, we began asking people to register their attendance online, and we've stuck with that. Make sure you know whether and how your church tracks attendance, and if there's any role you will play in that process as an usher.

Most churches will ask ushers to do a head count of the worship participants. We ask our ushers to wait to do their head counts just before the sermon begins and to try to do it discreetly. We want to make sure we allow any latecomers to find a seat before we count, and we don't want to cause a distraction by standing in the middle of the aisle visibly counting heads. Our ushers can either walk into the usher room to record their count, call it in on their radio, or text it to the Head Usher.

Offering

Many churches pass offering plates to collect the congregation's financial gifts. Pre-COVID-19, we did too. After the sermon, the pastor would call for the offering, saying something like

> Our ushers are now going to come forward again, as we have an opportunity to give back to God through our tithes and offerings. If you have a prayer request, place your prayer request card in the offering plate as well, and we will be praying personally over each one.

Our ushers paired up, one on each side of the section, walked to the front of their section, and began passing the offering plates down the rows. Usually, they would have two or four plates or baskets and would alternate rows so that half the plates were going in one direction and half were going the other. This let them collect from two to four rows at a time, which helped this element of service go more quickly (an important consideration if you have multiple services).

In some churches, two ushers will bring the offering plates (or a few of them to represent the whole) up to the altar and present them to God with great reverence. In most cases, the ushers look toward the cross and hold the plates up to present them to God, and then place them gently on the altar. This is meant to remind the congregation that while these offerings do support the mission and ministry of the local church, they are also an outward and tangible sign of our commitment to God.

Some churches use brass (or brass-looking) plates; others use baskets, plastic buckets, or bags. Some churches don't collect offering as a worship element, but instead encourage members to place their tithes and offerings into boxes at the exits. During the COVID-19 pandemic, we switched to mostly online giving, but we also have locked acrylic boxes near the exit doors so those who still want to use cash or a check can drop their offering in on their way out. Review the guidelines for collecting the offering at your church with your team leader and follow the leader's direction.

Communion

As an usher you may have a role to play in serving Communion during worship. For guidelines and suggestions, see the section "Special Services" on pages 25–27.

Children and Families

Many churches today have soothing rooms or nursing mother rooms for parents with infants, but what do you do if a guest has a very active (or vocal) child who's a little older? Please don't suggest they leave the worship space or take their child to your children's programming. It is stressful for the parent as it is; to suggest that their child should be taken out can be heartbreaking and may result in them not returning. New families may not be comfortable dropping their child off in your children's ministry until they're comfortable with your church. Children may have anxiety about being separated from their parents in a new place. Sometimes the parents are trying very intentionally to familiarize their child with church. And on occasion, let's face it, kids can just get antsy or cranky.

Be prepared for children who need some room to move or something to keep their hands and minds busy. We have a supply of activity books and crayons available at every entrance to our worship space on a stand at kid's eye level so they can grab their own on the way in. Remember that everyone is welcome—even wiggly, sometimes noisy, children. Our ushers are proactive, pointing out the activity books and crayons to children as they walk in, smiling, and making sure the kiddos know we want them there.

If a family decides to leave the worship space when their child begins to get antsy, let them know they're welcome to find a space for their child to move around, but they're also welcome to stay. This might be a good time to mention your soothing room if it also has toys and space where a child can move around.

Post-Service

During the benediction, ushers who are assigned to doors should head back toward the doors and stand ready to open them at the end of the benediction, to make it easier for the congregation to exit. Those not assigned to doors should stand near their sections and offer a warm goodbye to worshippers as they leave.

At the close of service, when everyone has exited, take a moment to tidy your sections, picking up any stray bulletins, lost items, and trash, so the space is clean and ready to receive the guests at the next service.

Finally, return any supplies to the usher room and depart until next time.

Special Services

Ushers are often asked to serve at occasions other than weekend worship, such as Ash Wednesday, Christmas programs, guest speaker events, and others. One special service that happens monthly for us is Holy Communion.

We offer Holy Communion in our chapel after every service each weekend, but once a month we celebrate the Eucharist in worship as a community. In some churches, the ushers might pass the Communion elements through the sections, using trays of little cups and plates of Communion host. In other churches, ushers might serve Communion as congregants come forward to receive. Make sure you're familiar with your role in Communion as an usher, if you have a role to play in that worship element.

In our church, we have a separate team of Communion servers, and our ushers are charged with releasing the rows in their section to go forward in a way that keeps things moving and doesn't allow a long line to form. They offer hand sanitizer to each person as they exit their row to go forward. If there is a person with limited mobility or other special needs, the usher will ask them if they'd like to be served in their seat and then will instruct the servers to bring the Communion elements to that person after those who are going forward are done. The usher will then tell the servers that their section is complete, and he or she will receive Communion before the Communion servers serve one another and replace the elements.

For Ash Wednesday, our ushers serve in the same way, inviting each row to go forward for the imposition of ashes.

You may be asked to usher at a funeral. Most of your responsibility here will be helping people find restrooms or other locations and ensuring there are plenty of tissues in the space. You might be asked to greet and hand out programs at the doors and to seat people.

These special services are sacred, and we ask our ushers to serve reverently. Ask your leader if special attire is required. At our church, Ash Wednesday, Maundy Thursday, and funerals call for subdued colors and dressier attire.

Occasionally your church may host a ticketed event. Our Christmas musical program is our only ticketed event, and our ushers' primary role is to hand out programs, welcome people, and help guests find their assigned seat. At community events, such as a guest speaker or a panel of speakers on a specific topic, our ushers greet and welcome people, help them find seats (and the restrooms) if asked, and help to tidy the space after the event.

Other Duties as Assigned

Every job I've ever held has had the phrase "other duties as assigned" as the last bullet point on the job description. The same is true for ushers. In some churches, ushers are the first to arrive and hold broad responsibilities for making sure the space is ready, including making sure the paraments are the right color for the season; the altar candles are ready to be lit; the pastor or guest speaker has water, mints, and other supplies they might need; or making sure there are tissues available during cold and flu season. These duties might also include making sure the current week's bulletins or other handouts are available at the doors, the lights are on, and the temperature is comfortable in the worship space. Talk with your team leader about expectations for ushers not covered here, and be ready to serve with a willing heart.

Tips for Ushering with Excellence

- Arrive on time; your leader is counting on you.
- Dress appropriately.
- Smile and greet guests as they arrive; assist with seating if needed.
- Know the order of service and be prepared to implement worship elements such as passing attendance notebooks, collecting the offering, and other special liturgical elements.
- Pay attention in the huddle and review the bulletin, if your church uses one, so you can answer questions that guests may have.
- Be flexible and stay positive when last-minute changes happen.
- Be aware of your surroundings, in terms of both who is around you and what is happening in the space.

- Take a head count of your assigned section(s).
- Know your church's emergency procedures for severe weather, a health crisis, or other emergency situations, and know what your church expects of you.
- Extend a warm goodbye to guests as they exit.
- Tidy your section after the service so it's ready to receive guests again.

Ushers play an important role in the church. They are responsible for not only welcoming people, but also ensuring that worship and special events run smoothly and providing direction to congregants in case of emergency. Ushers need a combination of people skills and attention to detail. Readying the space for guests, making sure all needed supplies are at hand, providing an excellent and welcoming guest experience, and implementing worship elements are all included in the usher's job description.

CREATING, LEADING, AND SUSTAINING A MINISTRY OF WELCOME

If you have just been made responsible for creating a ministry of welcome, you might be thinking, *Where do I even begin?* Maybe you're leading a hospitality ministry that needs some revitalization. That's a position we all find ourselves in at some point. It can seem like a daunting task, but if you take it one step at a time, one day at a time, you'll be amazed at what you can accomplish—especially if you invite a group of people who are passionate about hospitality to dream about it with you. And that's an important piece of the puzzle: not trying to do it alone. Hospitality is a team sport. Invite others to be ambassadors for your vision, to be role models for new people you recruit, and to help lead and maintain motivation in your teams.

At Resurrection, we use a model for volunteer management that involves four steps: Invite, Connect, Equip, and Sustain. We'll discuss each of those elements briefly in this section.

Creating Your Hospitality Ministry

First, define what excellent hospitality should look like in your context. We spent quite a bit of time defining and then refining our vision for hospitality at Resurrection, and you can find the details of that in a book titled *The Art of Hospitality* that I coauthored with my friend and colleague Debi Nixon.

Determine what roles are involved in your ministry of welcome. Those roles vary from church to church but always include ushers and greeters, which are the focus of this handbook. In your church the person who makes the coffee, the people who help direct traffic, and those who serve at your welcome desk may also be part of your welcome ministry.

Outline clearly your expectations for volunteers, both globally and for each specific position. Your global expectations (in other words, the expectations your church or ministry has for every volunteer) should be contained in a volunteer covenant. The expectations for each serving role should be documented in a ministry position description. This handbook includes copies of our hospitality volunteer covenant and our ministry position descriptions for ushers and greeters and our Head Ushers and Head Greeters.

One reason these documents are so important is they allow you to clarify your expectations for anyone who wants to serve *before* they begin serving. I learned this lesson firsthand when I was leading our Spiritual Gifts teaching team. There was one person on the team, our very best teacher, who never attended any of the team meetings, which meant he sometimes wasn't on the same page with the rest of the team. The other teachers began to resent the fact that this teacher didn't come to any meetings and seemed to follow his own rules. It was causing tension on the team. Finally, I invited him to meet for coffee and asked him why he never came to the meetings. His response: "Because you never told me it was required." We were able to resolve that issue easily, but another problem wasn't so easy to fix.

A few years ago, we had a greeter who was extremely negative. And unfriendly. And always had a sour look on her face. She was the epitome of the kind of person who shouldn't be serving in hospitality, yet she had been serving in this role for years. Have you ever experienced a situation like that? It's not fun. When our team began a renewed focus on hospitality training, this volunteer attended the training but didn't change her behavior, despite numerous coaching attempts. Ultimately, we met with her, reviewed the expectations for serving in our ministry and for her role, and told her we needed her to step down from leadership. That was a difficult conversation, and she claimed that the expectations for serving had changed, which wasn't fair. In reality, our expectations hadn't changed but were now documented, and we were committed to holding people accountable to those expectations because the ministry of welcome is so critical to building a healthy, growing church. The conversation with that leader would have been so much easier if we could have pointed back to expectations that were clearly explained to her before she began serving.

When you have laid this foundation—your vision for hospitality is clearly defined, you've determined the roles involved and your expectations for volunteers—your next step is to share the vision and expectations with any current volunteers first. You don't want to recruit new team members into a team that isn't living into your vision. That will demotivate your new team members faster than lightning. Allow your current volunteers an "out" if their role no longer fits them based on the new expectations. Help them find a place to serve that's a better fit for them. When your existing team is on board, you're ready to recruit new volunteers (if you need them). For us, recruitment is a way of life. People move away, they move into different roles, they need a season of rest.

Let's explore briefly how many volunteers you need. I suggest you have a greeter at every exterior door. You probably have one door that is your busiest, even if it's not your front door. Post two greeters there. If any of your exterior doors have a vestibule, use a team of two greeters at those doors too. If you pass offering plates or baskets, you should have enough ushers to have two per section in your worship space, so they can partner to collect offering.

You'll want to have enough volunteers so they can serve on rotating teams. Some volunteers may want to serve every week, but most don't prefer that. They want the ability to participate in worship on occasion. You might have two teams that rotate every other week, or four teams that each serve once a month. In our hospitality ministry, we have four greeter teams and four usher teams for each service, and they each serve once a month. We do have some volunteers who want to serve more frequently, so they're assigned to multiple teams.

After you've determined how many additional volunteers you need, you're ready to recruit. This is the **INVITE** piece of volunteer management. It involves assessing the opportunities you have—places where individuals, families, and small groups can serve. Part of it is conveying the value of serving in the church. It means being intentional about promoting and communicating your needs.

We've found that we need to communicate two things effectively. First, we need to communicate clearly that we are inviting them to join us on a mission. Always communicate invitation rather than desperation. Second, we need to invite people into something that is fun, is accessible, will help them grow in their faith, and will make a tremendous impact on our guests. That's a lot of messaging, so we try to communicate some of it visually through photos or video, and some verbally through either text or messaging from the chancel. For example, we'll use photos of our volunteers smiling and having fun on the screen behind the pastor as he or she says, "We need four more volunteers for this service. If you're a people person and you can serve once a month, we need you."

Sometimes people ask us how we recruit, and the answer is: *every way we can*. We use chancel announcements, requests in the email newsletter, and pre- and post-worship slides, maybe just like you do. We've found that partnering with other ministries is often helpful. For instance, we'll attend one of our student ministries' events and invite students to serve. Or we'll ask parents to serve with their children to model for them the value of serving in the church. Or we'll invite small groups to serve together. One important piece of any recruiting method is making it easy for people to respond. This can be by providing an email address or phone number for them to use, asking them to fill out a form with their contact info and drop it in the offering plate, having a table in your lobby with current volunteers or team leaders for them to talk to about serving, or if you're recruiting in your email newsletter, including a link to an electronic interest form. We've often used Wufoo forms, which are free and very user-friendly (www.wufoo.com).

The most effective method of recruiting is still, and I believe will always be, the personal invitation. If you know someone who you believe has the gifts and talents needed in a specific role, tell them that. Most people are flattered. They often respond, "You really think so?" That's when we invite them to come one time to shadow a veteran volunteer and just try it out. No strings, no long-term commitment. And then we go out of our way to make sure they have a great serving experience. We encourage our volunteers to do the same thing, but to invite the new person to serve directly with them one time (shadowing), so they're serving with someone they know, which almost always makes the new person more comfortable. One of the ways we prepare our volunteers to do this is to ask them to share why they love serving in two or three sentences. Most of the time the results include statements like "I made new friends, feel like I'm making a contribution (or giving back), and get to make a difference in at least one person's day each time I'm serving." If your volunteers are able and willing to share why they love serving, others will be drawn to join them. For a new recruit's "shadow" experience, if they're not serving with a friend, pair them with one of your best volunteers, so they have an excellent role model.

When you have a new volunteer who's ready to join a team, meet with them to **CONNECT** personally so you both get a sense of whether this specific role might be a good fit for them. Review in detail the volunteer covenant and position description. Give them an opportunity to ask questions. Tell them you'll chat again in ninety days or so to check in, and if the role isn't a good fit for them, you'll help them find another role. This lets them know they're not going to get "stuck" doing something that makes them uncomfortable or that they don't enjoy, and it gives you an opportunity to observe and make certain the role suits them from your perspective too. If it doesn't, you can explain it in terms of expectations and observed behaviors that make you believe another role might be a better fit.

Make sure you **EQUIP** them to serve with excellence. This requires that you provide the training, resources, and tools they'll need to be successful. Training is important and should be ongoing. Rarely does being trained mean "once and done." Things change all the time, whether that means a new way of doing things, a new focus on an existing value, or a new vision you want to implement.

Equipping means shepherding and ensuring that volunteers are also growing spiritually as they serve. Equipping also involves identifying, equipping, and releasing new leaders.

One of the things we do to help equip our hospitality volunteers is invite them to attend a volunteer orientation before they begin serving. At this gathering we share with them our vision for hospitality and how it connects directly with our church's purpose and vision. We share stories and examples of how we've seen other volunteers serving in their roles positively impact the lives of real people. We share with them our volunteer covenant, which clearly outlines our expectations for how any volunteer would serve and interact with their fellow volunteers and our guests. What we've learned is that having a volunteer attend this *before* they serve both inspires them and motivates them to demonstrate excellent hospitality as they serve. Once they catch the vision, they become ambassadors of that vision, sharing it with others. As I mentioned, a copy of our volunteer covenant is at the end of this handbook.

Leading a Volunteer Team

Each volunteer team will need a leader. If you're serving in a small church, you might lead all teams associated with hospitality. As your ministry grows, find volunteers in whom you see leadership potential, and invite them to share leadership with you, with a goal for them eventually to lead independently. This will allow you to roam, oversee what's happening in multiple areas (or put out fires as needed), encourage and affirm other volunteers as they serve, and interact with guests. Having team leaders allows you an opportunity to model how the body of Christ is intended to work and to model excellent hospitality for your volunteers as you interact with them and with guests. They need to see you embodying the expectations you have for them.

Communicate with your teams regularly. We email our team leaders weekly with information they'll need to know when they arrive to serve. For our greeters, this information includes ministries or events that will be promoted in the lobby, events that might be happening before or after the service, who's preaching that weekend, any guests that we are expecting and where we have reserved seats for them, and finally, their tentative door assignments. For ushers, the email includes who's preaching, the order of worship, any special worship elements or instructions, any guests that we're expecting and where their reserved seats are located, and their tentative assignments. For both of these teams, we often include an encouraging story that one of them has shared with us, or an interaction that we've seen where they've made a positive impact or where they've demonstrated excellent hospitality. We always try to share a photograph to go along with the story if possible because a picture speaks a thousand words. We include a brief reminder of one of our principles of hospitality, which are shared earlier in this handbook (pages 4–7), and a reminder to show up at a specific time for the team huddle. Our goal is to get this email out on Wednesday, or by Thursday at the latest. This gives the volunteers a reminder that they're up to serve, as well as an opportunity to find a substitute if they can't serve that weekend.

On the day of service, gather the team together for a team huddle about ten minutes before they need to be in position to serve. Use this time to encourage, show appreciation, and share important information. The huddles typically take about five to ten minutes. We review the final position assignments, introduce any new volunteers who are serving, and let the team know who their emergency contact is that day. We share information they will need to serve with excellence, including any updates since the weekly email. We invite them to share joys and concerns and to pray that we will reflect Christ's love to every person we encounter. Finally, we share a few sentences of encouragement and appreciation and thank them for serving.

We started the huddles because we had learned we had some teams that were very close and others on which people served together but didn't really know each other. On the teams that were more tightly knit, with a sense of real community, they were gathering before service and enjoying snacks and conversation. We wanted all of our teams to experience that feeling of being part of a community. We developed a format for huddles that would lead to volunteers being encouraged, informed, and equipped to serve. When we first began our huddles, a few of our leaders were hesitant to lead them (and to pray aloud), and we sometimes had only a handful of people show up in time for the huddle. We began to provide a huddle outline (just bullet points) and a suggested prayer for the leaders to read, and that helped our leaders feel more comfortable. They were surprised at how eager their team members were to share their concerns and prayer requests with each other, how open and vulnerable they were willing to be. Over the course of a year, more and more volunteers began to arrive in time for the huddle, because it was building a sense of comradery that they hadn't had before. They began to feel like a real team.

Sustaining Healthy Teams

It is simple to **SUSTAIN** volunteers. It isn't easy, but it's simple. It requires your time and attention. Sustaining volunteer enthusiasm and commitment starts with you personally demonstrating radical hospitality to them. A big tool in sustaining teams is to remind them often how their role connects back to the vision and purpose of the church. It means learning their names and listening for, remembering, and asking about the prayer requests or family stories they share. Welcome them by name when they arrive, ask them about something they did or mentioned the last time they served, and watch their faces light up! It means saying thank you and showing your appreciation in tangible ways. It means rejoicing with them during times of celebration and caring for them in times of sorrow.

I've made it a discipline to send a card to every volunteer on our hospitality team who has a death in their family. It takes only a few minutes of my time, yet a few weeks ago I learned how impactful it is to the recipients. I was greeting at the door for one of our special events when one of our volunteers walked past me on his way to a Bible study. We waved, and I greeted him by name. He had gotten three-quarters of the way up a flight of stairs then turned around to come back, hug me, and thank me for the card offering my condolences on his father's death. With tears in his eyes, he said, "I just can't express how much it meant to me that you noticed my loss and cared enough about me to take the time to send me a card. It touched me deeply. Thank you." Me taking the time to send him a card made a difference to him, and him taking the time to thank me for the card made me more committed than ever to continuing this practice.

Showing appreciation may take the form of food. All volunteers love food! Many of our volunteer leaders bring snacks for their teams and make a point to celebrate birthdays together each month. Some teams rotate responsibility for bringing snacks among the team members. On special occasions, our church provides treats for each team as they serve as a way of expressing our gratitude.

Once a year, we bring all our hospitality teams together for a joint volunteer appreciation event. At this event, we provide a nice meal and an opportunity for them to enjoy conversations with one another. Our only agenda item is to thank them, and as we are expressing our appreciation, we share stories we've collected throughout the year of where we've seen them demonstrating excellent hospitality. This allows us to remind them of our purpose in a way that is inspiring and encouraging to them yet doesn't feel like another training.

When a volunteer wants to step down, whether that's to move to another role or simply take some time off, make their transition smooth. Thank them, take a few minutes to celebrate their service, and wish them well.

I believe that if you truly take the time to get to know and care for your volunteers, to demonstrate hospitality to them, and to recognize them for serving with excellence, you'll be well on your way to creating, leading, and sustaining a ministry of welcome. This is a ministry of vital importance to a church that desires to reach new people, grow, and remain healthy.

A quote often attributed to Maya Angelou sums up why we practice radical hospitality: "I've learned that people will forget what you said, people will forget what you did, but people will never forget how you made them feel." Before a guest decides to get connected into church, they first have to feel like they belong, or at least feel the potential for that. Guests return not because of what we do, but because of how we made them feel, and that starts with the ministry of welcome.

APPENDIX

Appendix

Greeter Position Description

Greeter Role

Greeters are leaders in the church, tasked with offering a warm welcome to everyone who walks through our doors by showing radical hospitality. This ministry is vital for helping all our guests feel welcomed and to start to create a sense of belonging.

Greeters are responsible for the following:

- Live fully into the Volunteer Covenant (see document on pages 43–44).
- Arrive at the designated meeting space forty minutes before the service to participate in a team huddle, so you can be in place at your door and ready to greet guests thirty minutes before service time.
- Model radical hospitality:
    ◊ Stand outside and open doors for our guests as they arrive.
    ◊ Make eye contact and smile! Greet everyone, including children and the elderly.
    ◊ Offer a warm greeting, such as "Welcome! We're so glad you're here!"
    ◊ Assist those needing a hand getting in the door.
- Stay at your door for the first fifteen minutes of the service. Our first-time guests are often the people who arrive late.
- Attend a quick debrief with your team after the service.
- Attend trainings as needed.

Every week you will receive an email communication from your team leader with information about what is coming up that weekend in worship services.

Schedule: Usually serve one weekend per month, thirty minutes before the service until fifteen minutes after the service begins.
Regular meetings: Attend team meetings approximately quarterly; annual training.

Appendix

Head Greeter Position Description

Head Greeter Role

Head Greeters are key leaders in the church, tasked with leading a team of greeters who offer a warm Resurrection welcome to everyone who walks through our doors by showing radical hospitality. This ministry is vital for helping all our guests feel welcomed and to start to create a sense of belonging.

Head Greeters are responsible for the following:

- Live fully into the Volunteer Covenant (see document on pages 43–44).
- Email your team during the week prior to your scheduled service. Remind them that it's your team's turn to serve, provide them with important information for that weekend, and confirm their availability to serve. If possible, include their door assignments.
- Prepare to lead the team huddle, using the information provided by your staff leader.
- Arrive at the designated meeting space forty-five minutes before the service to lead a team huddle. Encourage and affirm your team, share key information, and ask for joys and concerns. Pray for the joys and concerns shared and that your team might share the love of Christ with everyone they greet. Review door assignments.
- Model radical hospitality—serve as a role model to your team. Let them see you living into our value of radical hospitality.
- Assist in offering a warm goodbye to guests as they exit.
- Hold a quick debrief after the service, to see if any concerns or issues arose. Thank your team for serving.
- Attend and help lead trainings as needed.

Every week you will send an email communication with information about what is coming up that weekend in worship services.

Schedule: Usually serve one weekend per month, forty-five minutes before the service until ten minutes after the service ends.

Regular meetings: Lead team meetings approximately quarterly; annual training.

Appendix

Usher Position Description

Usher Role

Ushers are leaders in the church and serve in a significant role ensuring the guest experience during worship is exceptional through radical hospitality. This ministry is vital for helping all our guests feel welcomed and to start to create a sense of belonging within our worship space. Below is a list of usher duties:

Ushers are responsible for the following:

- Live fully into the Volunteer Covenant (see document on pages 43–44).
- Extend the love of Christ through radical hospitality.
- Communicate with your Head Usher about your ability to serve. If you're unable to serve, request a sub
- Arrive at least thirty minutes before the service to review the order of worship and section assignments and to participate in team huddle.
- Fulfill usher duties as detailed by head usher and staff:
  ◊ Welcome guests.
  ◊ Help guests find seats, if desired.
  ◊ Pass attendance notebooks, if needed.
  ◊ Pass offering plates, if needed.
  ◊ Clean up section(s) after the service.
  ◊ Other duties as needed.
  ◊ Offer a warm goodbye to guests as they leave the worship space.
- Attend trainings as requested.

Schedule: Ushers usually serve one weekend per month, thirty minutes before the service until fifteen minutes after the service ends.

Regular meetings: Attend annual training.

Appendix

Head Usher Position Description

Head Usher Role

Head Ushers provide leadership to an usher team. Head Ushers are key leaders in the church and serve in a significant role ensuring an exceptional guest experience during worship through radical hospitality. This ministry is vital for helping all our guests feel welcomed and to start to create a sense of belonging within our worship space. Below is a list of head usher duties:

Head Ushers are responsible for the following:

- Live into the Volunteer Covenant (see document on pages 43–44).
- Represent Christ through radical hospitality.
- Send a reminder email to your usher team during the week before you serve, including the specifics for that weekend's service, and asking for confirmation that they are available to serve or notice that they are unavailable.
- Prepare section assignments.
- Arrive sixty minutes before the service to prepare order of worship, section assignments, and be ready to lead the team huddle, where you'll encourage and affirm the team, cover the details of the service, ask for joys and concerns, and lead the team in prayer.
- Lead the usher team in the following duties:
  ◊ Welcoming guests / Helping them find seats.
  ◊ Passing attendance notebooks / Collection of offering, if needed
  ◊ Gathering and recording section counts.
  ◊ Cleaning up section(s) after the service.
  ◊ Offering a warm goodbye to guests as they leave the worship space.
  ◊ Other duties as needed.
- Attend and assist in leading trainings as needed.

Schedule: Head Ushers usually serve one weekend per month, sixty minutes before the service until thirty minutes after the service ends.
Regular Meetings: Lead Head Usher meetings twice a year.

Appendix

Volunteer Covenant

*The following is a sample Volunteer Covenant based on
the covenant at Resurrection, A United Methodist Church.
It includes our vision, purpose, and distinctives.
Adapt any or all of this to fit the needs at your church.*

As a volunteer at Resurrection, I commit to uphold and support the vision, purpose, and journey of this church.

- **Our Vision:** To be used by God to change lives, renew churches, and transform the world.
- **Our Purpose:** To Build a Christian community where nonreligious and nominally religious people are becoming deeply committed Christians.
- **Our Journey:** To know, love, and serve God.

I will honor the values, distinctives, and expectations of the Guest Connections Ministry.

- **Our Values**—To demonstrate radical hospitality by:
  ◊ Noticing
  ◊ Offering personal attention
  ◊ Providing excellent follow-through
- **Our Distinctives**—I will use these filters to make decisions:
  ◊ *Outward-Focused:* Our words and actions should make nonreligious or nominally religious people comfortable.
  ◊ *Hope-Radiating:* Our words and actions should create environments and interactions that enable people to experience the love of Christ.
  ◊ *Thought-Provoking:* We desire to openly share our beliefs with others while being respectful, kind, and gentle toward those who believe differently.
  ◊ *Bridge-Building:* Our desire is to say or do things that make it easy for guests to build connections with the church and with other people.

- **Our Expectations**—I commit to:
  - ◊ Maintaining a friendly, inclusive, and welcoming attitude.
  - ◊ Going the extra mile to provide a positive experience for our members and guests.
  - ◊ Attending training and asking questions regarding anything about which I'm unsure.
  - ◊ Confirming with my leader(s) or finding a sub and arriving on time to serve so I am ready to fulfill my role.

Volunteer Name (Printed): _____

Volunteer Signature: _____

www.ingramcontent.com/pod-product-compliance
Lightning Source LLC
Chambersburg PA
CBHW011254040426
42452CB00017B/2808